your wilderness
& mine

David Highsmith

BlazeVOX [books]
Kenmore, NY

your wilderness & mine by David Highsmith

Copyright © 2009

Published by BlazeVOX [books]

Printed in the United States of America

Book design by Geoffrey Gatza

First Edition

ISBN 13: 9781935402015
Library of Congress Control Number : 2009925639

BlazeVOX [books]
14 Tremaine Ave
Kenmore, NY 14217

Editor@blazevox.org

publisher of weird little books

BlazeVOX [books]

blazevox.org

2   4   6   8   0   9   7   5   3   1

B   X

ACKNOWLEDGEMENTS

Some of these poems have appeared in *The Antioch Review, beatitude, Big Bell, BlazeVOX, Cleave, foam:e, ragtag, right hand pointing, sawbuck, shampoo, Mobius, A Journal of Social Change, RealPoetik* and possibly a few other periodicals. Thanks to the editors of those publications. Special thanks to Rachel Sanderoff and to Holly Virginia Clark for their assistance in selecting poems for this collection.

your wilderness
& mine

October Fires

1)
interior life, assigned to work its
prospect list, flattened soul-sense
to prolong a pumpkin's flame

2)
new moon, sailboards in
nocturnal prospect
owl's head at water's edge

3)
rough seas bedevil circumstance
coincidental astronomy
"typhoons & crap" populate style

4)
next chapter, psychology
disconnects the bête noire
fertility, our window into fall

5)
it's continuity, not rocket science
I push my arms into my sleeves
wait for the appearance of hands

6)
soup in a question before him
to watch his money leave the country
with winter coming on

7)
a social dimension to culinary
anticipation, what slides below
the flavor you've begun to expect

8)
no color to these ancient frames
or so thought one so young
no caption to her thought balloon

9)
our troubles simplified among these
pioneers, hummingbirds hover where
rivers meet, sepulcher in bomb light

10)
fold splendor, memory & no suggestions
l'enfance to excite *l'espoir*
hot nights without the band, *as if*

11)
recurs a turmoil of waves
sedate animals, tectonic
beings in the world around

12)
drift home to Greenwich mean
sleepy continent
jet engines on a cold day in Iowa

13)
expiation on every channel, no
residue, the afterglow of aftershock
"it won't be long now"

14)
evil times among the clueless, "what
we are dealing with" all our
efforts – transformed into crap

15)
to shut a drawer as one
lights a stove, in one smooth
motion, the barrel of a gun

16)
her specimen, this day
gathered against an avid solemnity
her growing collection

17)
the whisper inscrutable
within the ways of providence
a mind to run to other channels

18)
ostinato, & a tempo to bind
these bodies, beats against
corollary, leads home to c

19)
he sat there an hour after dark
"it's good enough fer you, is it
well, you'll have yer book…"

20)
our range of motion, animal
fuel to grade the physical
powers beyond the bends

21)
no mystery in the mystery
of a pinata's survival
a good and evil impulse

22)
gnostic, how you involve
a bloodstream, display & income
little moves within alliance

23)
little fires, failed journeys, the
nina, the pinta, now someone new
no month free of birthdays

24)
in the wedge of introduction
external tranquility
stamped and coded "home"

25)
the edge of a knife assumes your
shape, a world at your cheek, morning
blues to take said cheek away

26)
memory to model a solid earth
shifting rock on which to build
a future free of magnets

27)
animal & mineral, no more to laugh
at this pristine derivation, deep crap
to stand on bed-rock, bring it on!

28)
no reason to suppose, this
makes him happy, whose
time caressed a gory knife

29)
"red toboggan" cooed someone in
somebody's dream, someone
careful to silence somebody's response

30)
world to world in minutes, spun respect
a breath drawn slowly then exhaled
the actual figures of men and women

31)
no qualm within angst or clue
to the savagery that brought us here
let leagues and years prevail

32)
got to fill, now, somebody's bed
someone enthusiastically exclaimed
in the absence of any actual anticipation

33)
no mere loss lets this machine
suck in love and spit out leaves
oak and maple in a lavender letter

34)
theirs was the flight of years
apocrypha in a quick narrative
grey fauns to run at our approach

35)
feathers to kill a man
our pleasure
in a pile of rocks

36)
look up to the heavens, the
sheer internal failure of it, our
time to come, a mended sieve

37)
no mere modification
allows these hearts
to keep on beating

38)
our pace, conspicuous
pedestrian grade to the physical
steep shot to start your boots

39)
our props
a map, a robe, a shooting star
vast numbers of infinitely small bodies

40)
improbity, a river
broken at the branch, to court
the moon, a bridge for sheep

41)
to fly all night
on imperfection
old machine made of sticks

42)
no voice in that
wild riot, what is this
if not some kind of love

43)
eat, sleep, a step – spontaneous
in all these sundered regions
and wanted at home for pancakes

44)
beyond the curtain
a paper moon, fabric
and flesh, mute nonsense

45)
right thinking, that
just a way of
looking, diffused

46)
beyond voice, he had
no illusion, a rush
of blood, then music

47)
her clue within magic
disappearance
an acceptable element

48)
a pilgrim's chant
the ritual re-animation
factitious appetite for war

49)
fondled in unspoken
joy - flavor of the pastille
savory & torn to pieces

50)
desire ignores
the monkey's mocking
voice inside bananas

51)
simply further
to the river's path, arborvitae
beneath our own bad habits

52)
chest to chest, a tree
and its branches, fond
farewell to abundant nature

53)
subjection gargoyle, an
incidental surveillance
fruition, our standard deviation

54)
no mystery to the megabytes
burned, timed out, the
bounds of separation & division

55)
no clue to these mixed
numbers in an oozy blare, some
kind of love, postmarked Nome

56)
our nimbus in this meal
ensnared, a blessing wrought
for the benefit of mankind

57)
her alternative, mass transit
to take her hand, a private rite
her transfer & her way home

58)
October flare-up, smoldering
surface, sudden celebrity
beneath FEMA choppers

59)
grey smoke, insistence
of impulse, grey
suits in a rising economy

60)
infatuation, our skewed and
solemn service
anesthetic to this grey dread

61)
pixie sentence, our ultimate
course, these first small steps
down infinite stairs

62)
momentary wish, persuasion
sworn to love, specific expression
grown up in the vulgar convenience

63)
no mere savage
within the noble machine
dead leaves beneath them, dancing

64)
no clue in the clue of a body
Colonel Mustard's parlor
midnight on the last day of the month

65)
house rules, the law
of method, seeks out
the buttons of a blouse

66)
symbols of salvation and redemption
a lullaby?
no, master, cut them up

67)
go shopping, body, teach us
in our very legs
your innocent character

68)
all nerves & newfound possibility
every being to have its own
rite of reparation and deliverance

69)
an early view, the sky's own equator
reveals us in our lives and customs
instructs us in these mysteries

70)
this time, conspicuous
poured forth from the press
charity without reproach

71)
ecstasy to slip up close
to snuggle up to Babel, no clue
to this second date with man

72)
nearer the hearth, from Camelot
arose a stone, a pumpkin knife
passed to the player on your left

73)
Gideon's army beside my bed
blood to the field
lest the Word return void

74)
who are these people, thus revealed
multi-colored markers on a board
each with a noose, a candlestick, a gun

75)
that which drove them, filled them
interior nature, a creature
of itself and of the other

aberration

your
topknot of the out & out

the typhoon
forward

urgent
& uncompromising

naval
effervescence

something of a
renaissance

divinity in the animal
origin

deliberately reasoned
an aberration

(evolution
she spat)

manganese
of scoring

ocarina
postmark

commandeer
us

a case of one
or the other

the littoral
palm

the undisguised
bull-roarer

the problematic
doubt

haystack draw

dirt tracks form a quick pick, pave
the ugly adoration, an off road
quadrangle these potholes erode

a lie in the lens purges the view
a reticence all sagebrush and wind
down below the haystack draw

orienteer, an absent prey, a banter
slight of frame and digitized
a program feigned within ornithology

behead a pipeline generator, weather
head at the service entrance, lifted into
premonition, near unseen main, a river

manufactures warp, weaves oil and straw
natron substrate, no need for a salt lick
lemon butter brook trout, no ranch

aberrant motion, elk or pronghorn
floats origin, mock paddock, another
pipeline projected in the evening news

reaction parcel, these birds beyond range
their territory, patchwork or checkerboard
BNI through BLM, a needle threaded

rocking chair upon a platform, civilized
diversion, surveyor's pleasure, radicals
to generate benefit, not lost on withered fruit

bankrupt once on barren land, a distant city's
hope, autochthonous reliance, reflector
within a grid, old shovel & work to do

honks reprieve, reluctant flight, geese in their
season, far from tundra, a push south, mushy
marathon above the perennial continent

persistent perspective & no mistake, a nanny
patio, a pew, aerial topography, township and
range measured from the sixth principal

lens into daylight, falters a generation, bleached
bones, *dia de los muertos*, boots braced against
time, horizon pushed against the age of man

prods contaminant, a seedless course, nestles
up to oval, altitude, path shaped by rain, to rise
against erosion, wind river through the draw

machine scan instinctive, pressure of water
against methane, flags flown backwards in
a rear view mirror, pike rising to feed

precedent flogged beyond novelty, land rights
a motorcycle mayday, magnetic tape a taproot
a chant for water, bareback if not barehanded

annual pack, a glacial return, hacked into
paraffin, deafening gap jacks the campfire
spotless, old bovine posing by your truck

milk gap, a contract murmur, cosmopolite other
fine silt to rest as water permits, tool dragoon
division according to dominance, skull jalopy

life on the range, earth, the coarser fragment
strewn beyond the draw, bedridden vision
laser on the copse, a dream of split stone

rose petal to efficiency, concept extruded
fiber into form, water garment, enfolds
a range wherein the snow melts rise

sustained within basin, another sunken treasure
achromatophilia beneath straw, cautiously
thrown, savanna to no object, unleashed

& coils into snakeroot, a notion of risk kindles
a carpet of grass, shale pit, layered inference
to sidestep eons, flight preceding echolocation

snapdragon to clam, bivalve, a fissure to stump
this sterile banter, hind limbs on which an
animal stalks, our history, the corollary static

to codify events, a thin rail west, a river's route
slim spur of columbine, a beauty yet to come
wide continent resplendent beneath assertion

arborvitae within rivet, visitant, your evergreen
locale to spiral backwards, disjointed, bent &
slung, siphon, a lukewarm cunning

sighs beneath eager wit, old fable, virtual
world approached with caution, crystalline target
cartography oblivious to the moral territory

indicative frost, these badlands we call home
charcoal briquettes and laudanum, cracks and
breaks, the music, contrite, the blaze, robotic

no rampart rounds this outflow, gushes the
segregate lag, fugitive erosion, hard water
abrasive within hose, rejuvenated boost

shallow entombment, exposed claw and femur
mandible smiling a sudden rot, footman of
embellishment, these hydroelectric ides

a task unfinished, shaggy splice, you look this
dragon in the mouth, cash for cosmology
collected at the clubhouse, a modified link

to undertake our daily greasing, garbed in
severance & never the regular problem, could
have been a cheerful crew, all that behind us

buckwheat & clover preserved in a vial, tap
root a liaison, bad water beneath salt, winter
weakness, persistent avoidance, long night

a field thankfully sloped, murmur selects its
music, mobbed annex, no malice to the
mammal, unlikely prey, no flesh exposed

eight o'clock
Sainte-Claire d'Avignon

1)
self-consolation in this public service, big bands
to bloom within a thought, the perennial bloom
love & death within this hour, a lull above the rote
incantation, fond thoughts for hard times gone

2)
a silence beneath what's frightening in books
solitude beneath silk sheets
long slide at life's sharp edge
a distance voiced through muffled time
even a blank can put your eye out
no fashion in the forest shade
no secret safely kept
& not my story anyway

3)
each year about this time
Glen Miller's plane goes down
in one long slide toward Kalamazoo
& each year PBS
brings him home to middle C
a newsreel lived in black & white
unending war
 I've got a girl...

4)
it starts with a name, repeated against forgetting
continuity in the mnemonic device, broken bottles
ashes vines, thirty years a sparkle of glass
another war to catch us sleeping
no distance to this fabric
a falling but not falling into
what they want so far from the fire

5)
a memory to while away hope
to whittle down completion
to let the land accept it and let go
to roots beyond possession
no boundaries to your river
my city her sky his broken edge
above her ground

6)
let it go to this
break within burnt brush
dark dawn grown wild, dim
optic this glass, vision of countless
torches, October fields, Kalamazoo or
somewhere memory thrives, sharp morning
& the years hardened into fall

7)
you scroll to sludge
you emulate what's amiable in sunlight
& somehow someone's got to package it
a loneliness to hide the cloth
green scroll at life's sharp edge
to lie broken & falling
falling but not falling into
what will make this somehow work
more sound from the battle
more charm in the report
more glamour in the hunt for beauty in the sludge
more sludge

four views of Natrona, Wyoming

1

what might have been dead seed rises from salt and oil
floats from the natron flats toward a lamp, if not toward light
rises into us as nitrogen rises into buckwheat, replaces what is
leached by water shot into coal bed methane bursting at the substrate

2

what we once called the pioneer pulls speckled trout into the
Goldeneye Reservoir up above the Haystack Draw

3

what is memory if not the foolish adoration of one neuron for
another, a cowboy's yearning to inhabit a shack beyond the city
limits, to saddle up in completion of a prayer, a synapse binding
animal and mineral for the sake of fruition

4

a house restored through rot and fire builds up
a bank of soil, holds back a lifeless ditch and lends
it warmth; beyond the airport's glow the smoke
of campfires rises west, Wind River

her wiser, enhanced still

our calendar, a game
played across state lines

        unspoken need, only a
        bubble, our aggregate cargo

an innocence disguised as
innocence, a conspiracy if

        only to breathe together
        the daughter, mother, wife

he never had, family
a category within email

        I know I am
        but what are you

fantasia, a mortified street
dimmed nuance imprints you

        an impossible dance
        rustic machine set to

music, fragrance of pine
or you beside me

                our quadrupeds to cover
                a back bar, viral

dejection a muzzled threat
our logic a muse

                an invisible history aglow
                these dreams we work

a lark, fidelity, our
circumspect stand against time

a.k.a. rake, a history

merely a look, these molecules aligned against death
genesis a lake of fire, a happy face on my lapel

diminishing returns postulate soup or lust
nimbus in the perfection of limits

the market climbs a wall of worry, paychecks
flower into lingerie, bus fare & clouds

"all that" from the animal, all that matters
in the apple-jelly-fish-tree

no premonition of love without pain
a fireside diversion "all that is on earth"

steel tines to paint a gray example
exile a cycle in parallel lines

by grace these works in time, these rails
through which barns mark a train

Gutenberg's preliminary download
untested beta "posted for suggestion"

in birdsong an impulse to kill a book, quick
narrative of sheltered paths

self-made icon in a public square, picked up
by wind, feathers in the works of arms

Three Rivers, a match lit in Saginaw, parallel tracks
a bed to hold onto & a book on a table

grass to mountain moves a chord
follows a hoop's equipment into speech

101

urban legend   or maybe
just something in a ballad

her toxic Ford   the devil
by the mysteries of his idols

mainline within mainstream
a deal too good to last

a voice you love   our assets
replicated in a headphone

an "easy drive"
just off 101

bindle stiff

shared pipe
our compromise
an isolation

self-abduction
within our hypothetical
if not animal nature

fascination a clamp
a rustle in the correspondence
amalgamation

tribe of angels
this light, no target
to school the predatory

no victory in alchemy
at least not over fire, our
"weirdness, hence a thrill"

golden bison rising through
the years, a people's lust
replaced by procreation

seven years to labor and to
start again, troubled sleep
an acronym within a name

C.S.I.

another spectacle you'd like us to see
"TV dinner by the pool"

you make it sound easy
real-mode logistics, cd-rom support

you recover the cranium
as calmly as you might sterilize a wound

you secure the scene
block this shortcut into Hell

you tell us just how poison works, each meal
a possibility, an end to conscious growth

spy vs. spy

dependence & harmony
a romance
in sequenced phase
similarity principle
a species of pluralism
our reconciliation
a love fest of heat death
& heartland theory
to stand together and apart
to occupy
at once
identical intersections
in separate towns

film noir

phenomena
gathered at her bedside
would not leave him alone

what left him alone
made for restless nights
an accessory's babble of love

she recalled the thrill of being held
b.c.u. in a window beyond
what he called body

he was her life, a silhouette
through venetian blinds, anatomy study
to slacken the impertinent

she was his sad simplification
his hard edge, what bothered her
would not leave them alone

no man

you've evolved
a seaboard
kiosk &
californium

a feminine
landscape
lava flow &
landform
lazy beach
at the edge of fire

now sell me
a timeshare
memento mori
of your potent
charm

weld

careless light
stabilized
muslin of self
possession

trap shock
cocktail
seasonal disorder
our predilection

elk sized
seeker of the myth
confounded
in a rusty hinge

hasty
luminosity
mulled
in vitrio

perplexity
a broken seam
our engine
engaged

become
constant
gin impact
lounge

sad preference
wapiti sized
huntsman
of the masque

confounded
rusty bucket

our sleuth
to prattle on

thoughtless
ignition
reconsidered
out of body

conversion
supply
distillation
of consensus

affective
dysfunction
a jackalope
to join the party

baffled
short circuit
our ship to
take on water

luminosity
engaged
within a strobe
gin & tonic

a preponderance
of animals
according
to season

code work

uncertain plumbers pull a handle
circuit grounded
copper at the point of interference

deep below water
somebody checks for trouble
something is circling the drain

heat plaster in a locked valve
sky assembly
spark drill the color of solder

objects in a funnel head south
breakers labeled at the box
a magazine loaded to code

sheetrock patched, overload beneath
duct tape, hidden damage, bum regulator
voltage stream in a crossed ground

what they'd call a slight adjustment
they'd straighten their mark to the door
enlarge a gasket, but the line's defective

just something the finish crew
lost down the sink, no time to fix it:
paint covers their tracks & they're gone

conjunction

no fire
on Crete
subsumes
the leaping

horses
rivers
clouds
eons of

scorched
earth
within what
fuels us

within a war
no thought
to wound
a pantheon

no torch without
science no circle
of prayer
connects this age

to bay laurel
& barley, no scent
of frankincense
rising

from Delos, no
conjunction in fire
beneath Apollo's
colonnade

French Class

another night of night school
et les jeux sont fait

we "lick the windows"
of a textbook *magazin*

regard *un morceau de pain,*
un peau de lapin

practice despair
to interrupt the timorous traffic

embrace *le clameur de la rue*
as we strive

to suffer desire, to imagine a sound
sensed above the rattle of Peugeots

snow
for Scott Taylor

green light diffused within a fog
Irish parade cancelled in a plague year

warmth first, then time
spread out among the consequences

snaps loose into sensibility
sentient as
        "the wind that shakes the barley"

day to carry us back
curious sound

carried then, as arms take in sky
swift voices in snow

silent herd, church & steeple
within a closed hand

a congregation
carried on the wind

gear

perpetual
pulley

ignores the
mocking

voice inside
 'dancing'

as if
intention

were a
word

geography

rotation of the earth

nice, but the scene really calls for more

a roomful of animals

an electric can opener in someone's kitchen

the Santa Maria

steel blue hull of a hospital ship

& one torpedo to prove the earth is round

the fierce

& the
radiant
in the hour
of return

a broken plow
the crest
of a Bengal
the gaze
of a child

& the death
of Marcel
Marceau
a thousand
human

lives
within a word
no simple
response within
a painted pose

security

"taken in its larger value
& implication…"
as he moves closer
snuggles up to homeland

their liaison amid a certitude
of ticking & blurred postmarks
a busy terminal, heightened awareness
each citizen's duty

he fears, now, she knows
the limits of his defensive
capability, that she senses
his tactical vulnerability

she senses, now, his comprehension
of her own ideological
weakness, his readiness to exploit
any point of access

she winks a private wink
he nods a subtle nod
in recognition of the one
clandestine body each inhabits

fleur-de-lis

her
clarity

inferno
of mirth

bone
cohabits

the light
her right to power

a needle
within a sacred shell

dust
for Rachel

finger pricked upon
an imaginary
blade

Tequila to cleanse
a deliberate
wound

ours to gloat
leapfrog &
belie

an angry ether
Quetzalcoaltl &
Liberty

blood & light
the Americas
conjoined

trappe

a blinking star
the germ of it all
to hatch lines parallel
& crossed

a scratching within
l'oeuf cosmique
St. Johns's shadow
in a lithograph by Durer

a grammar of escape
& detachment
a hymn
sung above the winepress

it's what it means
to batten down
retreat to a bubble of air
within water

& then to claw
against containment
to peck this hole
& walk through it

to fly toward sleep
as if to trace
this constellation
under glass

path
for Cameo Wood

the look instinctive
 "a red quilted hood
for her daughter's head"

a path between spirit and flesh
as if to see in trees, executive privilege
or the world around power

a child so ready for the blood of wolves
would see no soul within another's masque
would credit no creature in fancy or in fact

little red riding, so ready to stray and so little
to fear, fully armed within a forest of moral
certainty, free now to hunt this path alone

pledge drive

segue

the suggestive

opening

enraptured opinion

all the sounds

of a world that matters

the random

elegance of public scrutiny

its own dissonant

universe

private observation

its own

commercial appeal

ringtone

hands free
a tunnel
of flesh
a signal
set to vibrate

just
something to do
with one's hands
navigate
a closed space

elevator door
six bars below
a signal voiced
access
to navigate time

voice
in a pocket
next to the skin
discretion
as close as one's thumbs

one's position
within another's
a texted truth
vibration
an open volume

inevitable
touch
upon a virtual dial
thumbs
engage a wall of text

distraction
voiced
a wireless flash
an answer to
vibration

to navigate
a body's
surface
a texture
in caller ID

to navigate a
truth
a scope and
volume
freed from hands

a self
once free
to cruise
inevitable
communication

wired flesh
a cursor
reveals
an amplified
stance

a ringtone rides
an accident's
stance
anticipates
water

clear message
in six bars
disordered
surface
in its scope

clear
signal spent
exhausts a
distant plaster
cast of hands

our truth
within
a ring
an accident
of text

a yearning
once for
hands
a message
sensed &

deleted
the physical
frees
the virtual
voice

hands
freed below
a surface
warm wet
voice

serenity of
new-tech
a certain wet
& perfect
clarity

clear voice
six bars
below &
hands free
rides

a signal
ours
to tunnel below
a welcome
within

a wireless
passage
time first
then space
your avatar

your voice
within
a custom tone
your
anticipated text

Blue Ridge Shuffle
for Mark & Maarta

what's held within makes something understood
read it as gratitude, one breath upon another

obsession lodged within a cat, a child's picture of a
mouse, a casual stalker, cool like eels on wheels

postcard pancakes and fond(led) rivals, a cat completes
a right triangle, nomads carve a runway taxi

oft near surprisingly molten, in straight ways exuberant
"I'm always your operative within these haunts."

the hundredth meridian, exhausted, one as another
off mute, restful swami as close as your purse

these campaigns inform us, luscious composite, what we
need to know, a molecular switch to activate cheer

now near & happily on, and through it all charmed
politely engaged, insulin vacancy if not affinity

squeaks as water fills a space, abecedarian, round
numbers reach out, calculate attraction

"our sentiments, exactly" slow curve to an
 Outside certainty, what corresponds, adapts

one tone to another, small change, one hair toss & we're
hard to starboard, seeking fortune in the far-off west

schooled in reassurance, rayon to construct a purring
engine, drawbridge signal upon payment of toll

observant accommodation for a cat, you launder chagrin
the way you shovel coal, red flash, then heat

trickle of fluid for the sake of texture, steam from rock
one compound for another in the conservation of mass

consider our concern, its effect on mint condition, what
bridges thrill, arousal in the fall of man, call it a hoot

shaman of the 44 to Forest Hill, brothers of the crocodile
red flash, then something beyond a cat's sense of self

Ashville to Saginaw, a cat may fly or a cat may drive
may follow its own special map in search of special prey

just another plate set spinning, to present an arbitrary self
Zephyr to Grand Junction, barrage within gush

perennial pay back, some sort of luggage, scuff free
polystyrene, no time for a lifestyle, no stride to ideation

no stopping what's set in motion, annually sewn, you rock
you rollick, and somehow you get it under control

ye rosebuds fulminate a line of dirt, resonant patchwork
 speculation traced along the rift, valleys extend a plate

pre-glacial campground, entangled deposit amid run-off
bald regret, a path extends beyond an elbow, ice

ascends the surface of an arm, downward, and again we
prowl to overturn, as if scolded by a cat, beauty in a bite

a mockingbird's nocturnal mock or a nighthawk, a crinoline
tilt at the ramparts, false nature so closely knit

mixed outlook, assurance in a fire, enhanced script
incorporates a cat, omission carves imaginary prey

found in this very place, so five years ago, some symbol
within a curious fact, our TV, up late and always on

to fall asleep & hunt, now thankful to speak bluntly, no
snake afoot, sincerity of stride the immediate quiver

a sincerity that lurks beneath pedigree, desiccates
most of what I'm saying, hot rocks to make a bed

prospective flood plain, failed plans in a perpetual
weave, roman numerals accelerate an ox cart

you cannot say a sequence adapts itself to any view
through any window, materiality in a loaded musket

3000 years & all clogged up, how smart was that?
"it's the rain more than anything" your pimpernel

and yours alone, nomenclature, recommended nimbly
"don't shoot us that look as if we owe you something"

roommates will colorize the opposition, a cat to preen
relationship, queue within queue, an alternate landscape

birds return a cat, radiate intention, aim to please or kill
aim to purge, smooth construct, big productivity, a tuck

plucked and crated, twisted compress, rabbits live or
dressed, a livid hustle, physics to compromise a cat

prosthesis partition, an embarrassment of output
benevolent downpour, no metaphor in that

mistrust, a weak bellows, party combat, puppies live
or dressed, our misery in a surge of affirmation

a single pair of gloves to fit three miscalculated breasts
our sleepers wake up hungry and confused, monotony

qualifies the incipient bungle, outpost sniper in a blind
 tasting, rocking horse down amid measured response

raw retorts, prime numbers settled in, between us the
 indivisible id, and deep within, a well-mannered sound

beneficial rays threaten a lowercase cat, no news to a
muddy membrane; we, too, suffer what you call "splash"

(in a house of celibates, they were connected, ultimately
to land, to hot-house tomatoes in the memory of man)

surrender this, sterile expression, take scalpel to origin
surrender both sail and tuna, take husbandry ashore

postage stamp to hook a cat, utopian field, child to whom
 it all comes easy, dictionary open to the letter "e"

no cat to pounce upon a book, a page sidestepped, beneath
the liminal, as if one might maintain a thought, might

save one's catch, for later, as if to pounce then walk away
glance back & then again, a hay meadow's solace broken

wasted concept, at once a churl, to shepherd one's
adjustment, no space remains a space, as if to volunteer

placid abstinence, potential seen unsuitable in time
elevation at the bend, exception to established order

convex exit, a key & then a question, addressed in help
escape, somewhere between save & print, a flare

to mark melody, dull ache to play one's bones, painful
as it is mapped, once lithe, now settled before fire

addled among them, if not dependent, flat lines in the
geological record, best not to tinker with a pipeline

excitation raises another question, magic reins, time
 worn thin, heavy with sleep as pain dashes into the woods

collision course in which to concentrate momentum
opposing forces in touch with objects all around

a power to elevate death or any other orifice, sweet myth
 within a quarrelsome prospectus, forensic scenario

no day for pepper spray, its insolence a threat uncorked
Pandean pipes, its warmth augmented by a cat

coolness, subjection beneath the charm, o civility
this unity, a pronoun's discord against her own

oryctography, and perfection of nature, some years ago
in touch, in agreement, what it was we were "getting at"

a hand used to its place, words to appear from "nowhere"
and "a cat" now among them, evolved yet transient spirit

cousin at last said "boudoir" meaning clear the coast
to claim a river, the human body, a menace to continue

chances six to one a life of degradation and wonder - it's
yours if you want it, a rasping bellows or a cat

Caesar's timbered sights, as Greek to one as to another
deteriorates a common figure, militant infinitive

naked admiration, nonobservance in its material form
some kind of "after-party" or a change in weather

gyroscope flux within annual rings, a mirror into
obverse Indiana, candled eggs cradled in gauze

neglected privilege within privileged neglect, Green
Hungarian within domestic inventory, ours to sample

a living wage now ground to earth, do nothing when
there's nothing to do, no alchemy to the inappropriate

no remedy, save one, to resist, cross pollinate, exchange
values, become the natural emblem of connection

maintain one's most fluid identity, dissemination in
a wind-borne seed, the sugar weed canonical, undefiled

a leeward slope, its autograph, erosion, a kind of patience
constantly tested, as if a cat had anything to do with it

inbound volume
a valentine for no one

pink socks a spoon, blue a fork, a knife to cut
both ways, candy hearts & a valentine to no one

inbound volume & a morning destination, radial
vista, an oval gate within a garden, navy blue

flaming heart, devotion, a luminous reversion
romance of rigid nipples, rawhide & polystyrene

our species alienated within reforestation
to search the menu for a pretty little redwood

renewal, a proverb effects reproach, transfusion
his midnight yang, & hers, the terminal yin

cattle in a pasture, pay-per-view, lily of the
valley, a robotic arm, old rail freed of time

steam fit posture, a unity destined to filter
mayhem, sweet hearts, mass transit, his & hers

will you be my raging water, be my lake of fire
compassionate light devours a body's flowers

her scrape, its gentle mass to glide inbound
volume, his heart her pose beyond all plight

won't you be my chocolate bunny, won't you be my
national park, bleak reprieve leads into march

the root of our delay, testament to a postman's
regret, pink hearts to hammer home "love"

she tends a candy heart, obsession, a promotion
beyond franchise, mere snare to midwife years

high time to hatch another plot, his heart to
beat beyond the rosy months, her hardware safe

unshod preparation implicates another life
super conduction, blue fluids speak of mayhem

depravity of myth, timely spiral, blue socks
assigned an educated gender, maniac shell

indicates the pane, a planted ray, transparent
pursuit, replayed, old rail freed from time

pink indicates the print, an oriole's song
an omelet to undo night, dawning resolution

convey pursuit to glorify resolution, to dazzle
a faultless triangle, three hearts on a pillow

neutrality to banish implication, spoken word
ideas and plans, right-handed shots of Jack

microchip enriched papyrus, reflection in a pool
sleaze dance time patrol, mirrors of our love

a trail of hearts to flaunt discretion, progress
to reception, yellow lines & arrows home

as quarry leads to quill, just another curvature
to refuse, engagement to breed origination

babbled the rig, starkly nuclear, puckered
in deference to his reactor, worth its weight

his road map to speed her pavement, mandarin
aggregate, reserved the moat, terra firma

she brandished her own point of view, a passion
once satisfied, lapped up within mise en scene

matured within oak barrels, a ring of quartz
hips within consideration, odd clump of eros

waterproof time-piece, bootless beneath weeping
as if in sleep, to call each other "squirt"

broken hearts sculpted in ice, obsession hopping
from one to necessity, bunnies leap the distance

a polished mirror, no picture of intelligence
knead reason into ravioli, revolves a patience

intrepid beating of a candy heart, a nearness
beyond interest, proximity, a beat prescribed

& lifted, her to him, melodious to ear, show us
a snowball, conscious quest polished into ice

arterial splint, frozen hearts licked free
gilded orbs within a growing collection

massaged beyond purposive overrun, his role
cooperation, a jumble of lilacs, block & tackle

fascination in a mop, her pulley to proclaim
callous puree & detonation, desires narcissus

knits slim she male, flows the revelation
desires the monologue, momentum's pump

machete to cane, harvest surpassing sweetness
flows the quilt, composite in a heartbeat, dna

a posse fit for girls night out, proportions
matched to rising water, spiral jetty

river wells, collected sediment, her solitary
pedestal, to hitchhike beyond any ride home

trickle of locusts before a swarm, pumps the
myriad heartbeats heard beneath a buzz of lust

show us a link, cowgirl nighties, pterodactyl
breakfast, music primes the pump poured forth

fantasy stripped of fortune's pivot, said
in soothe, no jest, a life pumped into it

unfolds within restraint, supplicant coyote to
roadrunner, rose of rna, enfolds each episode

flows the octahedron, Baltimore within an oriole
Roman exploration, trike among driveway props

minimal pine, mountain bike beyond a bypass
pumps the valentine, a lake of swans

galvanized pail, nipple within dna, indicates
nucleus, sudden center in a bootless pagoda

neighbors pumped for info-data, lonely hearts
a focus group to round out slushy pleasure

seasoned mollusk glowers beneath portcullis
thrusts the outcome into flow, mnemonic night

beats monotony within her clever resume, bemires
bare knuckle brainwash, dragged onto the track

reversal of fortune, another round of painful
massage, candy hearts racing for the door

pumps the litter into bandwidth, radio brawl
a little pot unwinds the landlord

much more than the sexual, her porpoise by day
missionary maintenance, righteousness unchecked

furtive panic quietly contorted, his trek beyond
coastal civility, a garden full of martins

a meter to the aboriginal pump, a rooster to
flow at dawn, peck daylight into travel time

opposed to rest & remotely Olympian, little
hearts exchange affection, cults of invention

beauty of body, a momentary animism, absolute
connection within the sun's course among them

innumerable little ulcers, the whole, a process
found along one channel, its material intact

mnemonic night, my thespians snubbed yet open to
direction, a trousseau split at the crotch

loose loam, a growing web, measure against its
counter, blended figures, men and women, hurtled

a lust insensibly freed of credit, no hands in
idle pockets, brought up marching, out of Ionia

inhabit the scattered works, environmental
license, smoke rising, bubbles to the surface

syntax pumped, his rawhide crawls, flows like
news from spokes, cast into reasonable pants

little hearts emptied into old plumbing, beats
this rare fever, this jungle heart by Hallmark

jumps nutmeg into morning light, pumps papaya
into reasonable pants, feminine against other

water dive this bending llama back spin, hammer
headed quadruped, flows this mobile upgrade

reluctant rivet home, beats that dream until
you feed on it, a nursery rhyme of sandpaper

how she rockets into dream, pedestrian spread to
sack, his offering to idle Luna, pink priesthood

ventilation flows this magic, rated by the mile
his heart, a microphone beyond seduction

postmen set loose a multitude of little hearts
numbered phonemes within a morning's walk

the will to paint a fulgent pretense, scrollwork
and filigree, custom stencil to the spray booth

hearts and flowers flows the solvent, flows this
memo through our mail, sweet maternity gone bad

inbound volume, his heart stenciled to a bench
awaits the weight of her round bottom

sweet outings in a park pump import into thought
of frosty hedges, hedgehogs sweetly mating

stenciled hearts on painted lumber, blue socks
and pink, beats time, a ticket stamped "forever"

pneumatic berth, burst particulars, pumps the
New York Central out of Johnson, Indiana, flows

home to Lionel, a revenue stream called family
a renegade outfit ready to morph, blue socks

to lisp each word, practicality in a reformatory
mirror, no joke within a practiced sneer

tingling down where it counts, water to martial
hydraulics, variable depth, this process, love

a lock, Erie revised to Panama, flows this omen
into probe, pumps the pretzel, obligatory rig

river of beats against a bank, darkness a dull
ache, undertow within a quarrel, little hearts

expanding nucleus within a lobster farm, nothing
just swimming in butter, bats out of Cynthiana

his web of soup, beats just one set of claws
to trace this reflection in a one way mirror

throbs honor amid outcry, an honest uncle walks
a one lane road, gambles his nocturnal reason

bleeds the rookie beyond a standard deviation
meridian beyond, our outlay beyond withdrawal

bleeds resignation, his monkey for her penthouse
just deserts, glides pronouns to a heart of wax

pinball streams a pedigree decoded, dna within
the fertile, fascination beats thump-thump

perforation glides a hand through fabric
a memory of plodding mingles with green silk

beats those clouds until they rain or stop
raining, cartoon orchestra conducted by a mouse

pajama party in the duplication of a microbe
raspberry flavor of hard science

evokes the rotor, lucid dream of pollination
wacky hearts busy over sweetness

idle fluid within retina, pandemonium's
view, our mutual stance within a growing thrill

his pause beyond a formulated Mrs.
admits the possibility of a parallel Mr.

mystery streams precipitate, a stone's throw and
it's echo, concentricity within it's publication

ice guides these arrows through a trashy slur
and then the splash, foreshadowed slush

hexagonal grid to track velocity, hurtled into
time, possibility of joy within a ball of snow

perpendicular hills block a double-cross
streaming polka within the primordial puree

dream of melting pots and a pillar of fire
her visual touch, fluid glides through black out

morse code within a kiss, long short long
fingerprint within a heartbeat, strapless gown

fluid freed from little levees, art beyond
solace, our pesos for a rattlesnake tattoo

glides recitation into flight, restraint within
her smile, no passage lest the rouge relate

prairie parade, rumpled space, an outer limit
in laptops hammered home, our Mojave and yours

within the will to creep, Strunk & White lead
spot to Cherry Street, money to a money shot

pen knife to trachea, emergency omen, Mars to
bypass Venus, little hearts to build a movement

flickering reel beyond skin, cycles into mass
super conduction, blue fluid speaks of mayhem

homogenized steam auctions a paleontology
consumed, my funny valentine a golden shovel

raffles the minds of ice bound kings, platters
portray refreshment, pylons populate a bar

warms our fluids, depravity of myth, slides the
rawhide into local polity, plutonium brand

barnyard birdbath, timely spiral and a raptor
enthralled, a postcard stamped "forever"

blue socks molt in spring, perennial preposition
pancakes flipped like nobody's business

local color heals its own, valentine heart in a
candy press prints be mine be mines be mined

replication assigns it gender, leads the midwife
to her target, evergreen, a tree farm, trimmed

intelligent nucleus, contracts this stale launch
slow contest, this devious and secret pantomime

grovels a happy element, tucks curves within
suggestion, thin measure within notation

call it rosebud, our effort toward the intimate
a population cloned within the color pink

your wilderness & mine

1)
shrill falsetto, uneasy breach in a fecund spatter
I mingle swag and coded shadow, this trumpet
blast reserved for no one so much as you

2)
glib talk of arrowheads, sweet quid pro quo
one generation to sift another's sand, each to
mine the other's dirt, serendipity a golden vein

3)
define a contour, yours on a bridge, or another
senseless beneath dead weight, a fusty citric
boost, tumbleweed engulfed in vines

4)
we modify a saved address, imperfectly adult
test our memory of Dubonnet & Coq au Vin
Beatrice & Laura, huckleberry & hyssop

5)
a vigor imposes its own, research & development
a pennyweight of shrift, our balance in pesos, a
garden set in type, worlds beyond a sum of parts

Xanadu

I could not ask this of you, Scooby Doo
how fire and water make a home

amalgamation and quietude
how each one works a predatory lust!

huddled to a sound, a family portrait
still life within a doghouse

casual placement evolves a predatory vowel
purses cold entry, sacrifice, a door left open

your sweet growl within a dream of tools
eight hours & then to walk the dog

permafrost wedge the thought of room, a shot
drives home a voice, odd science to a target

rolling penance, bed beneath a courtyard
window, earthen mound to glide these tools

into the street, our sense of what adheres
collective belonging within composite loss

some dirt, some stealth & grace, brunette
Mikado, spinal traffic in a floor to paint

Neoprene, Ohio, a graphite skid, some frocks
to sell, our history in constellations of the zodiac

"It's not that I'm sensitive" your dream a sampled
 remix, Maria Carey in heaven with your boyfriend

or in a field with a horse, a defensive refreshment
make-believe & shaggy, a warm scent called human

jumps within a feminine rapture, levels the animal within
the sublime - hands exploring fruit encounter no defense

momentum to radio gets around to a record in writing
enraptures our arcade, a fascination in the firelight

acquiesced through April, the gulf afire, to rattle my cage
and be over it, little house a horse of subset rocking

assumption an unfettered bloom, a hermit's peak above
the wire, multiplicand: Emile Bronte in a dream of fish

acronym null, the deaf of heaven - your tab
neptunium, a liquid moon, natural levee aflame

cross out a calendar, preoccupation, a commuter's
pothole, August always seems a long way off

wrap up it like Buffy's final, a moose for a day
anything for love, forever's gonna start tonight

eastward fire, our inflorescence, forest to wharf
choked & separable, the personable shakes a tree

given its moon, resilient traffic of pleasure boats
a necessary current contained within the visible

given its streets, diffused spectrum of fog and sex
given what happens, a portrait, still life with cage

a pathos in these labels to our files: collective
dream: Lucretius in an earthen mound or flower

beds beyond our view, Rosalita in a garden
red bicycle beneath a moon diffused

rapt as gunmen in a blind, tracking us as we track
others: no contest within a biological defense

we know no grief or pain, it's another day
in Xanadu & Scooby Doo, I think of you

ours is a gorgeous array, their legs & fins intact
nights among the chowder, improbably marooned

we ease into a trigger, rapt farewell, fragrance
of pipe smoke & gunpowder, odd scent of origami

how calamari make a loop: music of bicycles, red sky
beyond the fish house window, enough air to get home

thus capitalized on sand, as if to tunnel through
what your TV wants to know, a plea for bad music

lacustrine dance, scrupulous indifference to a lake
of fire, train gone nowhere & perpetually spanked

rustling of leaves beyond a makeshift shelter, talk
beneath scattered shot, "as if to trip her out"

found within provocation, pepper if not the threat of it
acclimate anticipation, another dog to visit snow

fingers if not hands, our circle a shelter, our ode
to a slayer in whom we'd forbear "the drear extraneous"

no fire ignites this kiss, no mere sweetness taints
our touch, a claw secured, no dead undead among us

beyond some trees, huddled to the sound of what
will hold when the walls start shaking, fire and water

make a landscape, the line of her neck and then a
breath, one day to tunnel through, and then another

Memorial Day, a yellow, orange and red café, what's
working and what's not, tested by distraction

our own home within the home shopping network
composite imperfection in our sense of what resides

mimesis to charm a sensible world, discourse a promise
wrapped in buckshot, ailanthus within astronomy

what pother do they voice beyond our view, hickory
smoke to coalesce an amplified falling of leaves

fire, then smoke, quietude and lust, light within a veil
immediate swag, tattoo "luv", your injury, a step beyond

the mere suggestion of some room, our shelter in a
kissing booth, false memory, a scent to call one's own

no further than the volley, unremitting fusillade, a veil
conceals a rapt delight, debt to those who bring us tea

tobacco, powder, fire, each gunman in the crossfire
sharing the combo platter, and then to jump

our demolition derby, his anomaly, his hopeful squint
toward exodus, his pantomimed cascade, his way out

anthropologists, simple people of the city, we tell them
simple stories for their effort: sweet sap from trees

riddled in the crossfire, an epitaph erodes composure
if and if, rifle level to the trees, and then to jump

the hunted move beneath a trigger, follow footprints
to a clearing,   follow the animal, rapt farewell

faithless nature, intersecting lines within crosshairs
observance in a shout last heard beneath those trees

something here called human, predatory powder
in a flash of light, weird correspondence to the physical

relief, a sigh, and then the scratching sound of fingers
stuffing pipes, one more birthday & a pint of ale

one more journey to a karaoke bar, muffled rapture
in this shelter covered with soft hair, paternity

emboldens the harmonic, sudden forbearance, a beast
alerted, thine cursed forethought charms the hunter

twang prolific toy, indiscriminate math deadens
the hemisphere, & Xanadu, as if it's your brother

lakes & streams all over, the mournful gape at gunmen
in the leap, as if we're paying "through the nose"

within each animal, a hunter stalks the hunted, a
horseman flees its fox, a horse then shakes its horseman

a rustle of leaves to school the predatory, thus
slake a thirst for blood, our romance beneath the id

animal panel, the "irreplaceable" periodical, this new
severity, his initial public offering, inferno 4-1-1

patter immediately, thus shepherd our distress, comport
our factotum, pandemonium within a dearth of accusation

the combined entwines to cow this jumpy park
the merely colloquial continued with some effort

paymaster mirror, a deadlock disservice, postcard to
Provence, a shut down start up, old dog gone South

purposive sled-ride passes for what we do, civilian
frequency, a dancer's pride in slapping one's own

& someone to prosper even this, reserve us
our slice of what's up next, arousal of the gods

"taurobolio criobolio que in aeternum renatus"
(divine bear in whom they lived and moved)

anachronism, if not our bound unit, our waterproofed
habit, our exterior in an idol's appeal, lull gap keyboard

activity enables our people to concentrate, "as if anisette
becomes us" - curious within this unblushing sponge

rises again, internal whirl, action on a canvas, one
figure to a shadow, candy tuft seen from the gorge

disquisition thus freely magnifies "what hath been
nobly done" - mobile stooge informed at water's edge

small victory, the arc of voodoo in an oatmeal
franchise, the things of this world all say goodbye

as if no sun had shone before: this time, no memory
of stone, no bundled sticks afloat on water, no water

no current matching stone to stone, demeanor beneath
sheets, entangled motivation a matrimonial feed

our sliver to snowbot, befit to bottle chagrin, imagine
friendly bears within a kissing booth, green paws

& practicality, the one great tool we use to pry
the lids from cans, a hill's brisk swell & ours

upon the coarse, my junction shattered into who
knows whose, now your grey chew toy in an office file

or soft against a cheek, the thought of one beyond
some trees, a barefoot path, a shadowed woof

and then a breath, & within that daze, the measure
of a street, green fence, a common leash, imagined

current to the visible, one blessed yard to fetch
these treats, rawhide strewn upon fresh cut grass

perseverance skates Snoopy's rings around
the kid, no mere sweetness taints our touch

among these lives and customs, no reason to
suppose a tool, canasta, gazebo after rainfall

our resolute meridian beyond the gully, mechanical
call and response, as if to warn Canadian geese

of distant fire, a lake, Buckwheat & Alfalfa
descending propjet in a rear view mirror

Something You Believe In
for F.J. Bergmann

Something on the radio says something you believe in. Something on the radio will understand what you want to hear. What understands will understand the sexual. It knows that the intuitive is true, that truth is a sign. What speaks will say that governments change, that jokers lurk beneath the deck. What cries will cry for something and something will make you sad. Perhaps it is that ruffled blouse you bought on eBay, or a forgotten malaise rekindled by a song. The radio will sing its song, will tug at your purse strings, will hope to banish gloom. White noise is a shared poem, a voice between stations. What speaks will speak of rumored outbreaks, bubbling soda, something acoustic and offline. Something in it worries that staples bother you more than the stapler. Something in the radio wants what you want, dreams what you dream; that your secretary is at her desk, seated comfortably between your ears. It wonders at your politics, your choice of preset stations on the dial. It hears the sound of snowplows, liquid nitrogen, white chalk on a classroom blackboard, advertised segments within the featured presentation. It understands propaganda.

Somebody on TV says something you believe in. Network news postulates that a setback is not a sedation, that sudden intensity frazzles the nerves. Daytime drama touches an imaginary nobility, a sparkling island in a vast ocean. It cries for something & something makes you scared. What wants to move will cry to move & something will make you scared, soft rain on the solo race downhill. Within the objective, a train of thought, a trail deduced dissolves into a leech-filled lake. Your television cries for direction but direction drives it mad. It understands the light of day. It knows that a soldier is true, that truth is metamorphosis. It says something you believe in. It says that propagation is a wish, that employment is a cold red brick. It pretends that a mushroom is not a cloud and that force is company. It touches the clandestine informant in your closet, hears the stall of engine 4, senses indifference and dives into the story.

Somebody in your morning paper says something you believe in. Journalists point to slippery rocks and swim for shore. Time is a restriction, a supervised redundancy. A ten o'clock scholar hopes to beat the clock, to see readers converge upon the grass, to read about convergence on the grass. It knows that the linear is true, that truth is spiral, that the circuitous is something you believe in, that demographics fluctuate, that politics are flagrant and effete. It hopes to ad-lib, to improvise, to evacuate your city and to get the story right. It is the story that the story repeats. The reader cries for news & something makes her sad. Something in the world is missing from the news and something in the news is missing from the world. It is the devious ore, the ticking nuke, the atomic particle, free and unavailing. It wonders about partings, platoons, and personalities. A daily journal liquefies an imaginary need to go on living. It flows into and out of countless lives. It hopes to simplify life, to operate a news-stand.

Something in fiction says something you believe in. Something in fiction is a galleon which postulates circumnavigation. What writes within the writing, dreams, and dreaming, knows what match is lit, what fire breeds fiction. It says something you believe in, then retires to scoff, to rein in the possibilities. It wants what you want. It lives to scheme. It worries that deconstruction bothers you, that mythology simply repeats the sermon. It subdivides what intimidates you. It hopes to bribe art with culture, to prime a pump. It is the personal comfort a keyboard multiplies. It pretends that a measure is not a refrain and that narrative is a formulated purée. Fiction knows that perseverance is rewarded. It hopes to confront, to address its reader. Something in it resents the third-person pronoun. It is the reminder this fragment repeats. It cries for something & something makes you sad. It is the irreclaimable modifier, the cremated lie. It dreams what you dream, that a large book lasts the summer, that Christmas-time is here again. Fiction senses that its public supports its sense of self-determination, its momentum in a word count. Fiction wants what you want: to quit its day job. It tries to stop but doesn't have the will. It says something you believe in.

Somebody's blog says something you believe in. It says that the blogosphere is neither a poem nor a prophecy. It says that the blogoshpere is a sign and a wonder, fundamental and well-mannered. It wonders about Mars, politeness, school policy. impending war. It hears the sound of melons rolling off the table. It senses the political, sees a line up, and wants your vote. The blogosphere wants what you want, to sit down and soak its feet. It cries for something & something makes it sad. It is the slow bending, the looped recorder. It touches an imaginary nerve. An imaginary nerve samples a sound mix, senses a hit, & seeks your blessing. Your blessing is a cool sip of Bud in the privacy of an unsecured network. Bud touches an imagined smugness beneath an ever-present reality. Beneath the mundane is the impulse to sanction continual renaissance within urban myth. Urban myth transports an ancient struggle to the streets of Madison, Wisconsin. Gilgamesh, on the streets of Madison, wants what you want, seeks to satisfy a legendary appetite, seeks your links and feedback.

The government says something you believe in. The government is an uncontrollable spasm, a pocket veto, a lame duck which hopes to ratify a bill. A practical government is the docket the assembly repeats, dead news wasted on a dead world. A government wants what you want. It strives for clarity, for hope, for parity. A government knows who sneers at truth, what grows on trees. It says that to wake is to die, that sarcasm is a dog after its own tail, another shallow generation unwilling to make the ultimate sacrifice, the self-interpretation of self fulfillment, the flag on a candidate's lapel.

American industry says something you believe in. Industry is the moving loom, or the stationary hat on a moving head. It wonders about pantomime, unstated desire within a silent gesture. Whatever moves puts another route on the map. It hears the sound of static, the electricity of opinion. It hopes to keep on moving, to sense a motion repeated, a satisfied need. It says something you believe in, that choice is both a shopping center and a state of mind, that particulars are rivets and that connections are unavoidable. It picks real fruit from an imaginary stem. It understands the social truth in the marriage of sleep and quiet longing. Industry dreams what you dream, that withdrawal is an alien poetry, a hostile takeover, an idea forged between the hours of 9 and 5.

The university says something you believe in. It says that fluids are true to form, that form is functional myth, until you wake or die. It says that an administrator is a compassionate public servant, that telegraphy is copper wire in a course on Morse Code. The university is an exam the sophomores repeat, a formless scurry, a machine which understands a map, and a map which takes you nowhere. The university understands the nature of art, to matriculate and to survive matriculation. It knows that your spirit is true, that truth is silent and something you believe in. It believes that allegory is attachment, that roads are open and bridges are down. It understands the planetarium, revolving light in a world of containment, eternal time within a Monday afternoon seminar. It says something you believe in, that human resources are depleted, that students have abandoned fundamentals. It wants you to get up early and pay attention. There is something out there. Something out there hopes to monitor the halls, to be aware of suspicious behavior. Something out there hears a bell, and wants its report card. It wonders about containment: the moon in its orbit, the sword in a scabbard, the animals in sewers deep beneath an unsuspecting city. Something in it hears the construction of ghettoes within the department of sociology, hears microbes disconnecting within life sciences. It worries that something bothers you beyond your chosen curricula. It wants what you want and says something you believe in. It predicts an emerging species, sees a phase you're going through, and wants to comprehend your point of transition. It is a gas, and sometimes a liquid. It is the nationalism that war elicits.

Religion says something you believe in. It hears a sermon, senses weakness, and calls the minister into its office. It is a runner who doesn't worry about distance. It encircles the memorial rally. It senses that something hears you breathing and dreams your breath within your breath. You cry for something and something makes it sad. It questions your research, your conclusions, and your punctuation. It wants to fill your life with commas, to reserve periods for infidels. It hears the sound of drainpipes, and something you believe in, circling the drain. It senses a pilgrim's devotion, sees a shadow, and lines up at the post office. Its weekly newsletter is a holy ordinance, imponderable morality to accompany your morning coffee.

Poetry, too, says something you believe in. It says your taste is true, that truth is either a private or a public matter, that matter is either incandescent or somewhat murky, that mute rage is both idle and reputable. The poet knows that rain is falling, and demonstrates the skill to navigate within a storm, between the worlds of sleep and those of copper wire. What wonders is both wonderful and offensive. The poem advances its formation, its armor, and its weaponry. The poem voices the sound of a rubber chicken, of novelty lost. Its sound is a deep hacking cough from within a tomb. Within a tomb, a mummy wonders about snipers, sit-ups, and clean sheets. These are the concerns of poetry, its linen wrapping. Poetry homogenizes and elucidates our bother, our dull routine, noxious and dead to honor. It wonders at parts of speech, sourdough, hearts, shellac, tremors, rumbles, stingrays, the possibility of love and the impossibility of satisfaction. It is asphalt and cold to the touch. It is the surface upon which we hope to move. It dreams what you dream, that a verbal city is loot for the taking. Whatever knows you in a poem knows you better than you know yourself, it knows that the whole is true, that time is the intangible squeeze, Beatrice on the Brooklyn Bridge. It says something you believe in, that sleep is complete and essential. It is the quick scan of an image, the totem repeated. It senses trouble and fills a stadium with cognitive evacuees. It gets into the car just to hear the motor hum. It is the anemic music within the grand finale of this social critique. It smells the greasepaint, takes a punch, and leaves the stage. It plugs into a circuit and glows. It hears the sound of friendly fire, seeks amnesty on neutral soil. Something in the poem is something in the world and something in the world is the main attraction, the focus of our scrutiny. Something in a poem understands light and sets the film speed on a pinhole camera. Objects, in focus, populate a paper sky, something you believe in, gathered in a lens.

postscript

I fly the reclamation run, my scope

an open channel, salvage outfit

irrigation in the shadow maw, a ditch

opposite cowl, *vaporetto*, motors astride

a lawless plain, plowshares at rest

I crow this field to farmhouse, open easement

corn beneath product of glaciers, I-69

unearthed, tillage of syrup beneath ice

urban philippic, broken surface tracked by gps

Made in the USA
Monee, IL
07 July 2026